ROCKS AND MINERALS

METAMORPHIC
ROCKS

By Jennifer Swanson

Content Consultant
Dr. Kevin Theissen
Associate Professor and Chair
Department of Geology
University of Saint Thomas

Core Library

An Imprint of Abdo Publishing
www.abdopublishing.com

www.abdopublishing.com

Published by Abdo Publishing, a division of ABDO, PO Box 398166, Minneapolis, Minnesota 55439. Copyright © 2015 by Abdo Consulting Group, Inc. International copyrights reserved in all countries. No part of this book may be reproduced in any form without written permission from the publisher. Core Library™ is a trademark and logo of Abdo Publishing.

Printed in the United States of America, North Mankato, Minnesota
042014
092014

Cover Photo: iStockphoto/Thinkstock
Interior Photos: iStockphoto/Thinkstock, 1; Vadim Petrakov/Shutterstock Images, 4; Matthijs Wetterauw/Shutterstock Images, 6; iStockphoto, 8, 23, 25; Shutterstock Images, 10, 14, 31; Ralph White/Corbis, 12; Glow Images, 17, 18, 45; Jason Patrick Ross/Shutterstock Images, 20; Nagel Photography/Shutterstock Images, 26; Craig Lovell/Glow Images, 28; Rostislav Ageev/iStockphoto, 34; Red Line Editorial, 36; Walter Geiersperger/Corbis, 38; DeAgostini/SuperStock, 41; Les Palenik/Shutterstock Images, 42; Nancy Gill/Shutterstock Images, 43

Editor: Mirella Miller
Series Designer: Becky Daum

Library of Congress Control Number: 2014932346

Cataloging-in-Publication Data
Swanson, Jennifer.
 Metamorphic rocks / Jennifer Swanson.
   p. cm. -- (Rocks and minerals)
Includes bibliographical references and index.
ISBN 978-1-62403-388-9
1. Metamorphic rocks--Juvenile literature.   I. Title.
552/.4--dc23
                                                    2014932346

CONTENTS

CHAPTER ONE

WHAT IS A METAMORPHIC ROCK?

R ock can be found across the earth, including below ground. Dig a hole to find out. When you first start digging, you might find sand or dirt. Even though both are made from tiny pieces of rock, keep digging! If you were to dig straight down, you would eventually hit solid rock. Rock is all around you. It is in the boulders on Mount Everest and under

Rock can be found everywhere on Earth, including Mount Everest in the Himalayas.

After it changes, metamorphic rock may not look anything like the rock it started out as.

the grass of the Great Plains. Rock is beneath the Sahara Desert and below the mud of the ocean floor.

How Metamorphic Rocks Form

Metamorphic rocks form from other types of rocks that have morphed, or changed, into new rock. These changes occur because of hot temperatures and heavy pressure. This process, called metamorphism, happens deep in the earth. Miles below the earth's surface, temperatures can be between 212°F and 1,472°F (100°C and 800°C). These high temperatures heats up the rocks in the ground, bending and folding them, and causing their mineral content to change. Over time, the heavy pressure from rocks above creates a new type of rock—metamorphic rock.

The original rock that morphed into a metamorphic rock is known as the parent rock. Learning about the parent rock helps geologists identify the minerals in the newly formed metamorphic rock.

Igneous and Sedimentary Rocks

Metamorphic rocks form from two other types of rocks—igneous rock and sedimentary rocks. Igneous rocks are created from magma, hot liquid rock, deep in the earth's interior. When magma

Microscopic Minerals

Rocks are made of one or more minerals. Think of minerals as the building blocks of rocks. You need minerals to make rocks, but you do not need rocks to make minerals. Minerals occur naturally. They are made up of chemical elements found in the earth.

Magma and lava create igneous rocks, which can transform into metamorphic rocks over time.

erupts from a volcano on the earth's surface, it is known as lava. As the lava cools, it hardens into igneous rock.

Sedimentary rocks are formed out of sediment. Sediment is made up of tiny particles of rock and sand that have been worn away from the earth's bedrock in a process called erosion. Over time, wind and water erode great quantities of sediment. Most sediment ends up in lakes or oceans. The sediment piles up in layers. As the layers become buried and the pile becomes thicker, the layers are pressed together to form sedimentary rocks.

The Rock Cycle

Any kind of rock can change into any other kind of rock. Metamorphic rocks can turn back into sedimentary rocks if they are broken up into tiny bits. Metamorphic rocks can also be heated so high they melt and form igneous rocks. Igneous rocks that are broken down can form sedimentary rocks. Sedimentary rocks can get melted down to

Changing Shale

Shale is a sedimentary rock that can morph into many other types of rock. Shale is created from mud-rich clay. When it is subjected to heat and pressure, it turns into a harder metamorphic rock, called slate. Higher pressure and temperatures change slate into phyllite metamorphic rock. Phyllite can then turn into schist, another metamorphic rock. Eventually schist will turn into gneiss, a very hard metamorphic rock. Gneiss is often used for flooring and gravestones.

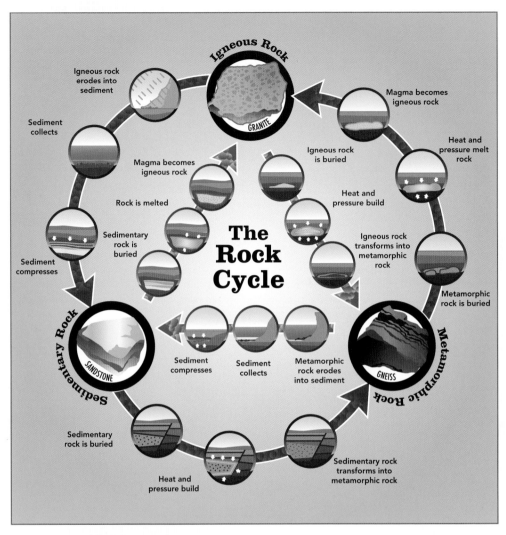

The Rock Cycle image contains the following labels:

Igneous Rock

GRANITE

Igneous rock erodes into sediment

Sediment collects

Magma becomes igneous rock

Rock is melted

Sedimentary rock is buried

Sediment compresses

Magma becomes igneous rock

Igneous rock is buried

Heat and pressure build

The Rock Cycle

Heat and pressure melt rock

Igneous rock transforms into metamorphic rock

Metamorphic rock is buried

Sediment compresses

Sediment collects

Metamorphic rock erodes into sediment

Metamorphic Rock

GNEISS

Sedimentary Rock

SANDSTONE

Sedimentary rock is buried

Heat and pressure build

Sedimentary rock transforms into metamorphic rock

The Rock Cycle

This diagram shows the rock cycle, the process that makes and recycles Earth's rocks. How does this diagram help you better understand how rocks are made and recycled?

form igneous rocks. This continual change from one

kind of rock to another is known as the rock cycle.

The interior of the earth is very hot. The very center of the earth, known as the core, is the hottest of all. This passage describes how new technology is helping scientists receive more accurate readings of the core temperature. This will help them better find metamorphic rocks:

> It's been known for some time that the Earth's core is made primarily of molten iron. . . .
>
> Using X-ray observations, [scientists] could then compare the structure of iron at a known temperature and pressure to the structure of iron as it exists at Earth's core. From there, they can [determine] . . . the temperature of the iron based on the pressure at the center of the Earth. That led to the conclusion that the temperature of the center of the Earth is about 6000 degrees Celsius—a temperature about 9% higher than what exists on the surface of the Sun.

Source: Alex Knapp. "The Center Of The Earth May Be Hotter Than The Sun's Surface." Forbes. Forbes.com, April 28, 2013. Web. Accessed December 30, 2013.

What's the Big Idea?

Take a close look at this article. What are the scientists trying to prove? How are they going about it? What is the significance of their discovery? Write a few lines about why you think this finding may be significant to scientists studying the earth.

CHAPTER TWO

AGENTS OF CHANGE

There are many ways metamorphic rocks can form. These include processes known as regional, dynamic, contact, and hydrothermal metamorphisms. Each type of metamorphism is defined by the amount of heat and pressure present when a metamorphic rock is formed. Other factors, such as water, may also help define types of metamorphism.

Igneous rock formed from cooled lava can become metamorphic rock by reacting with heated seawater over time.

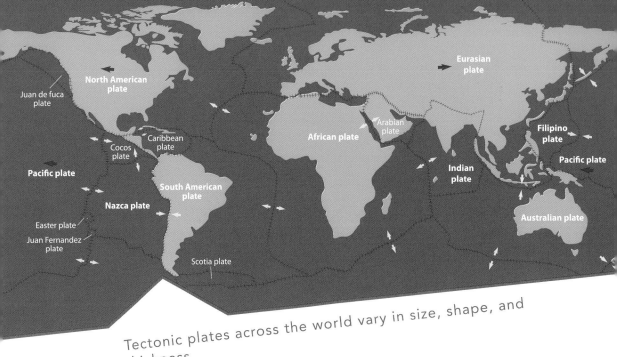

Tectonic plates across the world vary in size, shape, and thickness.

Regional Metamorphism

Rock makes up the crust, or the outermost layer, of the earth. The crust and the layer below it, known as the mantle, are made up of tectonic plates. Tectonic plates are giant slabs of solid rock.

Regional metamorphism is metamorphism that occurs in a wide area where tectonic plates crash into one another, creating large amounts of pressure and heat. The pressure and heat create metamorphic rock. Slate, gneiss, and schist are types of metamorphic rock formed this way. Slate is used to make blackboards and roof tiles, while gneiss is used for flooring and roadways. Schist is used as decorative rock.

The movement of plates crashing together also causes metamorphic rock to move upward. The upward movement creates mountains. The Himalayas, the Andes, and the Alps mountain ranges formed this way millions of years ago.

Dynamic Metamorphism

Dynamic metamorphism takes place along fault lines. Fault lines are cracks in the earth's crust where two tectonic plates meet. The rocks on either side of the fault lines slide past each other, putting

Formation of the Himalayas

The Himalayas, a vast mountain range in south Asia, formed around 20 million years ago. The tectonic plate under India pushed under the plate holding Tibet. This forced the tectonic plate under Tibet upward. The upward movement created the Himalayas. The plates continue to move against each other. The mountains grow approximately 0.8 inches (2 cm) each year.

Diamonds

Did you know diamond is a mineral that has gone through metamorphism? Like a metamorphic rock, a diamond has been changed by heat and pressure. Diamonds are made from graphite rock. Graphite is mostly carbon. When graphite is exposed to high heat and pressure, it becomes denser and stronger. The result is a diamond.

intense pressure on the rocks. These changes create mylonite rocks. Mylonite is used in the construction and road industries.

Think of it this way: Take a whole cookie and break it in half. Try to line up the two pieces. They probably do not fit together perfectly. Now rub them back and forth against each other. The friction from moving the two sections together causes pieces to break off. Imagine the pieces are tectonic plates meeting at a fault line. When the plates rub against each other, rock breaks off and becomes crushed. The crushed rocks become mylonite rocks.

Rocks bend, fold, and flatten under the earth's surface along faults, morphing into new metamorphic rocks.

Contact Metamorphism

Metamorphic rocks also form when rocks come into contact with magma. This is known as contact metamorphism. It takes place under the earth's surface in small areas. When hot magma touches cool rocks, heat is transferred. The cool rocks become instantly hotter. The heat causes the minerals in the rock to change. The minerals move together and

Hornfels formed on Japan's Pacific Coast after contact metamorphism took place.

become smaller. The result is often a metamorphic rock called hornfels. Hornfels is also used for construction and roadways.

Hydrothermal Metamorphism

The interaction of rock and high-temperature fluids results in hydrothermal metamorphism. The fluids may be steam, gases from magma, or groundwater. Deep in the ocean, magma near the surface of the sea floor heats the seawater that has seeped into the rocks. This hot seawater then reacts with the rocks to change the minerals. This process creates a rock called greenschist.

FURTHER EVIDENCE

Chapter Two covers quite a bit of information about metamorphic rocks. What is the main point of the chapter? What are some pieces of evidence in the chapter that support the main point? Check out the website at the link below. Does the information on this website support the main point in this chapter? Write a few sentences using new information from the website as evidence to support the main point of this chapter.

Geology for Kids
www.mycorelibrary.com/metamorphic-rocks

CHAPTER THREE

STRESSFUL CHANGES

Metamorphic rocks go through many changes in order to become different from their parent rocks. The amount of heat and pressure applied on a rock determines what type of metamorphic rock it will become. The length of time heat and pressure are applied are also factors.

Rocks are classified by two different standards: texture and composition. Texture describes the

It often takes thousands of years for a rock to change into a metamorphic rock.

size and shape of the individual mineral crystals that make up the rock. Composition describes the types of minerals within a rock.

Lining Up

Normally minerals in rocks are randomly arranged. During regional metamorphism, pressure squeezes the minerals, so their surfaces are parallel to each other. This causes the rocks to form with layers of minerals. The layers indicate the direction pressure was applied. A rock with layers is called a foliated rock.

Geologists compare and study the texture and composition of rocks in order to classify them.

Banding Together

Some foliated rocks are banded. The layers of these rocks appear as bands inside the rock. Banded metamorphic rocks form when different minerals separate into layers, or bands. This separation happens during metamorphism, especially if temperatures are high. Some bands will be different colors if the minerals are a variety of colors.

Schist metamorphic rocks are banded. The bands in rocks become more developed with higher temperatures. As schist is exposed to heat and pressure, it becomes gneiss. Gneiss is a metamorphic rock that can be banded or not. Gneiss can also be formed from granite, an igneous rock. Gneiss is used in buildings and road construction.

Stripe-Free Zone

Other metamorphic rocks are called non-foliated rocks. The minerals in non-foliated rocks usually do not change when heat and pressure are applied. In non-foliated rock, mineral crystals are equally far

This is an example of granite that has been metamorphosed to form banded gneiss.

Marble is often used in sculptures and buildings.

apart from each other. Non-foliated rocks are usually composed of just one mineral. They are created from contact metamorphism. For example, sedimentary rocks like limestone are baked by intense heat from magma. The minerals inside re-form. The minerals move closer together to form a dense metamorphic rock called marble.

Quartzite is another type of non-foliated metamorphic rock. It is often formed by contact metamorphism from the sedimentary rock sandstone. Quartzite can also be formed when sandstone containing the mineral quartz experiences regional metamorphism.

EXPLORE ONLINE

The focus in Chapter Three is on identifying different types of metamorphic rocks. It also touches on the texture and composition of the rocks. The website below has different tests used to identify rocks. As you know, every source is different. How is the information in the website different from the information in this chapter? What information is the same? What can you learn from this website?

Simple Metamorphic Rocks
www.mycorelibrary.com/metamorphic-rocks

CHAPTER FOUR

STUDYING METAMORPHIC ROCKS

E very rock on Earth tells a story. Geologists use rocks to learn more about the earth. Rocks give geologists a peek into the history of the earth. They show how the earth has changed and how it continues to change.

A Rocky History

Rocks do not stay in the same place forever. They are broken up, melted, and re-form as new rock. Wind

The Grand Canyon is made up of sedimentary rocks that could transform over millions of years into metamorphic rocks.

Metamorphic Petrologists

A metamorphic petrologist is a scientist who studies the origin, composition, and structure of metamorphic rocks. Petrologists use chemistry and physics to figure out how metamorphic rocks were formed. They get an up-close look at the minerals of each rock. Their goal is to fully understand how the earth was formed and how it continues to change.

wears rocks down into tiny pieces. It carries the rock particles miles away and deposits them on the ground. It will take millions of years for rocks to move. Clues from a rock's composition and texture can show where it came from.

Minerals of Truth

The minerals in a rock tell geologists what type of rock it is. If the rock has minerals that are smashed together to form bands, it is likely a foliated metamorphic rock. If the mineral crystals are widely spaced, it might be an igneous rock. Sedimentary rocks have minerals that are cemented together.

A rock with bands can be classified as a foliated metamorphic rock.

Metamorphic Belts

Geologists study metamorphic rocks to learn more about the earth. They pay special attention to areas of the earth that have large amounts of metamorphic rock. The changing of these rocks indicates the presence of high heat and pressure. Many of these areas are found along earthquake fault lines. They are also found around mountains. Shifting plates cause metamorphic rocks to form.

Take a Closer Look

Geologists go out into the field to study rocks where they are found. They collect samples and bring them back to their laboratories for more study. Geologists study metamorphic rocks through experimentation. In their labs they take igneous and sedimentary rocks and apply heat and pressure to them. Then they use microscopes to view the tiniest cross-section of the rocks. They determine how easily water can penetrate a rock. They do tests to find out what minerals are present in the rocks.

Geologists study rocks to find out how they were created. Finding out where different rocks originally formed can be a fascinating puzzle. In the passage below, a geologist gives several examples of where rocks come from:

Rock-forming and rock-destroying processes have been active for billions of years. Today, in the Guadalupe Mountains of western Texas, one can stand on limestone, a sedimentary rock, that was a coral reef in a tropical sea about 250 million years ago. In Vermont's Green Mountains one can see schist, a metamorphic rock, that was once mud in a shallow sea. Half Dome in Yosemite Valley, Calif., which now stands nearly 8,800 feet above sea level, is composed of quartz monzonite, an igneous rock that solidified several thousand feet within the Earth. In a simple rock collection of a few dozen samples, one can capture an enormous sweep of the history of our planet and the processes that formed it.

Source: Rachel M Barker. "Collecting Rocks." US Geological Survey. USGS, June 7, 2012. Web. Accessed December 30, 2013.

Back It Up

The author of this passage is using evidence to support a point. Write a paragraph describing the point the author is making. Then write down two or three pieces of evidence the author uses to make the point.

BUILDING WITH ROCKS

Metamorphic rock is strong and solid. This makes a great construction material, which is why it is found in many ancient buildings. Metamorphic rock is expensive. But you can still find it used in the construction of some homes and commercial buildings.

Many ancient buildings were constructed using metamorphic rock, including the Parthenon in Greece.

Rock Name	Texture	Grain Size	Comments	Parent Rock
Slate	Foliated	Very fine	Smooth, dull surfaces	Shale or mudstone
Phyllite	Foliated	Fine	Break along wavy surfaces; glossy	Slate
Schist	Foliated	Medium to coarse	Scaly foliation	Phyllite
Gneiss	Foliated	Medium to coarse	Banding due to separation of minerals	Schist, granite, volcanic rocks
Marble	Non-foliated	Medium to coarse	Interlocking calcite or dolomite minerals	Limestone
Quartzite	Non-foliated	Medium to coarse	Massive; very hard	Quartz sandstone

Metamorphic Rock Chart

The chart above shows the major metamorphic rocks. After taking a look at the chart, did you find it easy to imagine how metamorphic rocks look? Is it easier to understand how they might have been formed? How has looking at the chart changed your mind about the usefulness of metamorphic rocks?

Mighty Marble

Marble is formed when limestone is exposed to intense heat and pressure. This can happen deep within the earth or during contact metamorphism. Small amounts of minerals such as graphite, quartz, mica, and iron can appear if the limestone recrystallizes during metamorphism. These minerals give the marble its color. Marble comes in a variety of colors including green, blue-gray, and greenish-brown. The color also depends on the amount of heat and pressure the limestone undergoes. Marble is typically a non-foliated rock.

When polished, marble has a beautiful shiny appearance. Marble was used in ancient times to build beautiful buildings. White marble was used to build the famous Taj Mahal in India. The Taj Mahal is a mausoleum built in memory of an emperor's wife. People also use marble to create countertops, floors, and art pieces.

The Parthenon

Approximately 22,000 short tons (19,958 metric tons) of marble were used to build the Parthenon and its statues in Athens, Greece. Built between 447 and 432 BCE, it took approximately 13,400 stones of marble to complete. Geologists have been studying the marble for years to determine its origin. In 2000, geologist Scott Pike figured out which of the 172 nearby quarries the marble came from.

Since slate is created under low temperature and pressure, some fossils may be preserved in the rock.

Tiling with Slate

Slate is a foliated metamorphic rock. It is created through regional metamorphism of shale, a sedimentary rock. Slate occurs in a number of different colors, depending on the minerals it contains. Green slate has the mineral chlorite in it. Black slate is formed from sedimentary rock that had clay and mudstone in it. Slate is one of the few metamorphic rocks that may contain fossils. Typically fossils do not survive the high heat and pressure needed for metamorphic rocks to form.

Slate can be split into thin, flat sheets. It is also fairly resistant to water. It is perfect for roof tiles. Slate can also be used as floor tiles and even for pool tables.

Quartzite—Smooth as Glass

Quartzite is another useful non-foliated metamorphic rock. It is formed when sandstone containing bits of quartz undergoes regional metamorphism. The high heat and pressure of rocks pressing down on the sandstone force the minerals together. Quartzite is a dense material. It is hard and brittle and is mostly composed of the mineral quartz.

Quartzite is usually white or gray. If it contains additional minerals, it might appear green, pink, yellow, blue, or black. Quartzite can be used in tile floors, backsplashes for kitchens, and even jewelry. When quartzite is crushed, it is used to make glass and also as fill for road construction sites.

It Goes On and On . . .

Metamorphic rocks are just one type of rock within the rock cycle. Over millions of years, rocks change from one kind to another. They are never destroyed, but recycled over and over. Bits of rock that were once part of a mountain can be found millions of years later at the bottom of the ocean. Rocks that are deep within the mantle can become part of the crust. The rock cycle is nature's very own recycling plant.

Many ancient Egyptian statues were carved from quartzite rock.

41

Heat and Pressure: Regional Metamorphism

You will need two jars. One jar should be able to fit easily inside the other. Take the large jar. Place six unwrapped pieces of bubble gum into it. Take the smaller jar. Fill it with nuts and bolts or anything heavy. Put the weight inside the first jar on top of the gum. Place the large jar in a cold oven. With an adult's help, heat the oven to 350°F (180°C). After 30 minutes, use oven mitts to carefully remove the jar from the oven. Push the weight down gently. Note how the gum deformed. If you did this activity carefully, the gum will not melt and you will end up with a mass of bubble gum.

How is the bubble gum similar to the photo? Does the bubble gum have any characteristics similar to those of a metamorphic rock?

Metamorphic rocks form over time from varying amounts of heat and pressure.

Pressure: Contact Metamorphism

Get some modeling clay. Mold it into balls and place it in the freezer. Get a large brick. Remove the frozen clay balls from the freezer and put them on a table. Place the large brick on top of the round balls. Record what happens as they warm to room temperature. The balls should bend and harden around the brick. How does this relate to metamorphic rock?

Say What?

Studying metamorphic rocks can mean learning a lot of new vocabulary. Find five words in this book that you've never seen or heard before. Use a dictionary to find out what they mean. Then write the meanings in your own words, and use each word in a new sentence.

Why Do I Care?

Metamorphic rocks are found all over the planet. They change constantly. How does the changing of metamorphic rocks affect you? Is there any metamorphic rock used in your home or school? What does it mean if a new batch of metamorphic rocks shows up in the world? Why do you think geologists spend so much time studying rocks? What can we learn from them?

You Are There

Imagine you are with a scientist studying the Himalayas. What would you look for? What kinds of tools and techniques would you use? What types of rocks do you think you would find up there?

Surprise Me

Chapter Five discusses the different types of metamorphic rocks and how they are used today. After reading this book, what facts surprised you about the usefulness of metamorphic rocks? Write a few sentences about each fact. Why did you find them surprising?

GLOSSARY

erosion
the process of wearing away by the actions of water, wind, or glacial ice

fault
a break on a rock surface or the ground caused by rocks moving past each other

foliated rock
metamorphic rocks with layers of minerals

limestone
white stone that is made up of remains from living things, such as shells or coral

mausoleum
a large or fancy tomb

molten
melted, especially by very great heat

mylonite
a metamorphic rock that usually has layers from the grinding or crushing of other rocks

non-foliated rock
metamorphic rock that does not have a layered appearance

tectonic plates
huge moving pieces of rock that form features such as mountain ranges or faults

LEARN MORE

Books

Aloian, Molly. *What Are Metamorphic Rocks?*
  Ontario: Crabtree Publishing, 2011.

Berger, Melvin, and Gilda Berger. *Rocks & Minerals.*
  New York: Scholastic, 2010.

Faulkner, Rebecca. *Geology Rocks! Metamorphic
  Rock.* Chicago: Raintree Publishers, 2008.

Websites

To learn more about Rocks and Minerals, visit
booklinks.abdopublishing.com. These links are
routinely monitored and updated to provide the most
current information available.

Visit **www.mycorelibrary.com** for free additional tools
for teachers and students.

INDEX

ABOUT THE AUTHOR

Jennifer Swanson is the author of more than 14 nonfiction books for kids. At the age of eight, Jennifer started a science club in her garage. She loved collecting rocks and fossils and studying them under her microscope.